796.7
Hi

Monster Truck Drag Racing

By Martin Hintz and Kate Hintz

Reading Consultant:

Scott Johnston

Bigfoot 4x4, Inc.

CAPSTONE PRESS

MANKATO, MINNESOTA

C A P S T O N E   P R E S S
818 North Willow Street • Mankato, MN 56001

Printed in the United States of America.

Library of Congress Cataloging-in-Publication Data
Hintz, Martin.
　　Monster truck drag racing/by Martin and Kate Hintz
　　p. cm. -- (Drag racing)
　　Includes bibliographical references and index.
　　Summary: Describes the various kinds of monster truck drag races and the vehicles involved; includes a history.
　　ISBN 1-56065-390-6
　　1. Truck racing--Juvenile literature. 2. Monster trucks--Juvenile literature. 3. Drag racing--Juvenile literature. [1. Truck racing. 2. Monster trucks. 3. Drag racing.] I. Hintz, Kate. II. Title. III. Series: Drag racing (Mankato, Minn.)
GV1034.996.H56 1996
796.7--dc20

                                        96-22348
                                          CIP
                                          AC

Photo credits
Bigfoot 4x4, 14, 20. Mark Bruederle, cover, 6. Unicorn/Scott Liles, 10; Charles E. Schmidt, 12, 25; Dennis Thompson, 41; F. Reischl, 32; Aneal Vohra, 38. USHRA, 4, 8, 17, 19, 22, 26-30,34, 36, 42-46.

Table of Contents

Words in **boldface** type in the text are defined
in the Glossary in the back of this book.

Chapter 1

Truck Races

Monster truck racing is similar to other drag racing events. Like other drag races, monster trucks race two at a time. Each race is called a **heat**.

As with drag racing events, a Christmas tree tells the drivers to get ready. The Christmas tree is a pole with red, yellow, and green lights.

The light at the top of the tree is yellow. When it blinks on, the drivers move toward the starting line. A second yellow light flashes when the trucks reach the line.

Monster truck racing is similar to other drag racing events. But it is different, too. Car-crushing is an event for monster trucks only.

Then three more yellow lights flash. These lights warn the drivers to get ready. Sometimes a red light flashes. It means one of the drivers started too soon. That driver is **disqualified**. When the light turns green, both trucks race ahead.

The Races

Monster trucks do not race on a quarter-mile (400 meter) track like dragsters do. They usually race side by side on a 250-foot (75-meter) long track. Sometimes they race on an oval or figure-eight course.

Monster trucks crush cars. They do stunts. Crowds cheer when a monster truck does a **wheelie**.

Sometimes monster trucks race through mud and water. This is called mud bogging. Mud bogging is not as popular as it used to be. Monster trucks used to pull sleds full of weights, too. They do not do that anymore.

Crowds cheer when monster trucks crush cars.

Crushing Junk Cars

Car crushing is the most popular monster truck event. Audiences enjoy watching the big trucks smash rows of junk cars.

In a car-crushing event, the monster truck drives up a ramp. The truck is in midair for a few seconds. Then it slams down on the junk cars. There is a loud crash when the chrome, metal, and glass get crushed.

The air is let out of the tires of the old cars. Then the old cars do not move when the monster truck crunches them.

Drivers must be careful. A truck can flip off the row of cars and land upside down. A **roll cage** protects the driver. It keeps the roof of the truck from caving in.

There is a loud crash when a monster truck lands on a car.

Chapter 2
History

In the 1960s, off-road driving became popular. Drivers looked for rocks, mud, mountains, sand, and water. They wanted to test their skills and their trucks on rough ground.

Areas were set aside where trucks could race without hurting nature. Popular races showed that off-road driving could be fun and gentle on nature, too.

Some truck fans wanted more. Bob Chandler of Ferguson, Missouri, was one of these truck fans. Chandler was a carpenter who loved to fix trucks.

Bob Chandler got the idea to make monster trucks while customizing four-wheel-drive pickups.

Both friends and strangers brought their trucks to Chandler when they needed repairs. Chandler became so busy at his hobby that he did not have time for his real job.

Bigfoot

Chandler opened Midwest Four Wheel Drive in 1975. To promote his business, he customized a Ford pickup. He kept changing the look of the truck. He added larger engines and oversized tires.

Wherever he went, Chandler's truck attracted attention. He broke the truck often. One of his mechanics said it was because of Chandler's big foot on the gas pedal. The mechanic called Chandler Bigfoot. The nickname stuck. Chandler's truck became known as Bigfoot, too.

Bob Chandler added oversized tires to his Bigfoot monster truck.

Bigfoot grew and grew. Chandler added **custom-made** axles and huge tires. Eventually, the truck weighed more than 10,000 pounds (4,500 kilograms).

Car Crush in a Field

Chandler thought of new ways to show off Bigfoot. He wanted to try crushing cars. He secretly tried the stunt in a field.

One of Chandler's friends videotaped the car crush. He sent it to a **promoter** who loved the idea. Bigfoot did one of its first car crushes in front of an audience at the Silverdome in Pontiac, Michigan.

By the 1980s, Bigfoot had been in several movies. In the movies, Bigfoot did many stunts. Chandler drove the truck for most of them.

After the movies, Bigfoot needed repairs. Axles were broken, windows were cracked, and the hood was dented. But the damage was worth it. Many people became Bigfoot fans after seeing the truck in movies.

Many people go to see Bigfoot crush cars.

Bigger Trucks

Chandler made more Bigfoot trucks so he could attend more monster truck shows. Bigfoot V is one of the latest versions. It weighs 19,000 pounds (8,500 kilograms) and has 10-foot (3-meters) tall tires. Its tires were originally used by the army in Alaska.

After watching Bigfoot, some fans made monster trucks of their own. They gave their trucks such names as USA-1, Awesome Kong, Hercules, and Carolina Crusher. They raced each other at events across North America.

Rallies

A **rally** schedule is called a card. Car crushes are the events that make up most cards. Sled pulls and mud bogging used to be popular events. Today though, most monster trucks do car crushes, racing, and stunts only.

After watching Bigfoot, some fans made trucks of their own.

Car Crushing

Two monster trucks race against each other in car-crushing events. They usually drive over six cars.

The first truck to hit the cars does not always win the race. Many trucks break an axle or tip over before they reach the end of the row. It takes skill and experience to hit a row of cars the right way.

The cars come from junk yards. They are sometimes packed with bales of straw. That way they can take more pounding from the monster trucks.

It takes skill and experience to hit a row of cars the right way. Many trucks break an axle or tip over before they reach the end of the row.

Chapter 3
Making the Trucks

Truck companies promote their own models of monster trucks at rallies. Crowds cheer when Fords, Chevrolets, and Dodges battle each other. Everyone has a favorite model. They are happy when their favorite truck wins.

Each truck maker wants to have the best truck. They are always trying new ideas to make better trucks. Some ideas are borrowed from military vehicles made to run in the world's toughest **terrain**. Many ideas come from drag racing.

Truck companies put their names on monster trucks to promote their own models.

Engines

Drivers, mechanics, and engineers share their ideas. They put their experience together. Then they use computers to design the trucks.

The most important part of a monster truck is the engine. Engines have to pull a monster truck over many cars. Ordinary engines could not do that.

Some trucks use two engines. The first engine is in the front. The second engine is in the rear.

Superchargers are used to make the engines more powerful. Superchargers make the fuel burn faster.

Shocks and Tires

The first monster trucks needed many more **shock absorbers** than regular trucks. Some had four or six shocks on each corner of the vehicle. Today's lighter trucks do not need as many shock absorbers.

Bob Chandler's Bigfoot uses tires that are 120 inches (305 centimeters) tall.

Today's trucks use ladder bars. These are rods attached to both sides of the frame and to the axles. They support the middle of the truck. They take stress off the shocks.

Today's shocks are bigger than ever. Some are three feet (90 centimeters) long. Longer shocks absorb more. Fewer of them are needed. This makes the trucks weigh less. A lighter truck will race faster.

Most monster-truck tires are about 66 inches (168 centimeters) tall. Gary De Mauro uses 73-inch (185-centimeter) tires on his Towasarus Wrex truck. Bob Chandler's Bigfoot V uses 120-inch (305-centimeter) tires.

Names and Paint Jobs

Monster-truck bodies look like regular trucks. They are made of fiberglass, though, instead of metal. The headlights and grilles are fake. They are painted on.

Owners try to pick good names for their monster trucks. Some of the best known monster-truck names are Grave Digger, Black

Snake Bite is one of the best-known monster trucks.

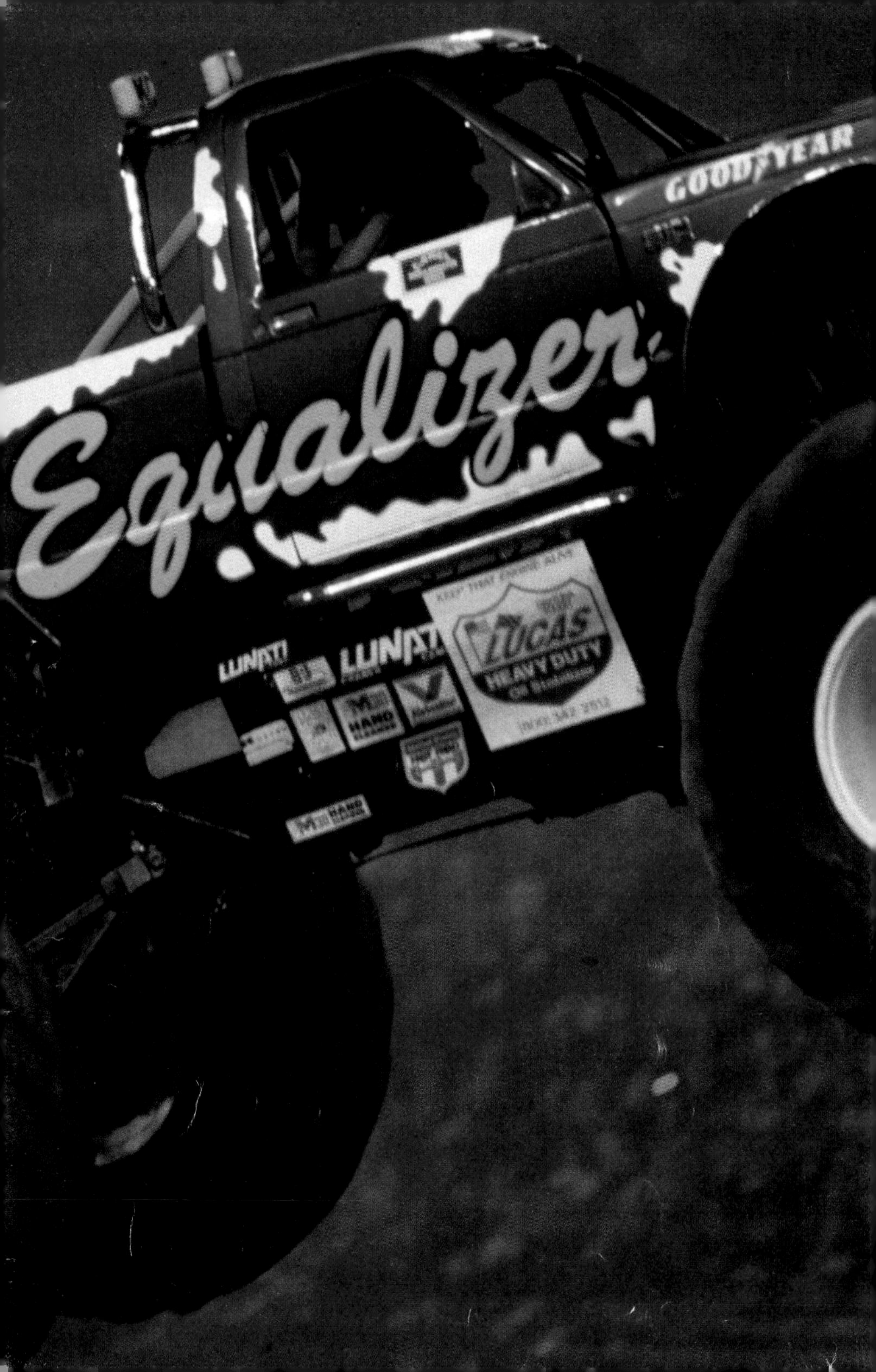

Stallion, Boogie Van, Carolina Crusher,
Overkill, Snake Bite, and Bigfoot.

Once the name is chosen, artists go to work.
They use special paint. They use a lot of it, too.
Exciting paint jobs are important at monster
truck rallies. Nobody forgets the looks of such
monster trucks as Terminator, Hawaiian Punch,
Star Monster, or Ohio Earthshaker.

Sponsors

It costs a lot to move a monster truck. The
huge tires need to be taken off the trucks. Little
tires are put on in their place. Then the truck is
driven into a trailer.

The huge tires are loaded in the trailer, too.
Several semitrailers, mobile homes, and vans
are needed to bring crews and equipment to
truck rallies.

Sponsors give money to monster truck
teams. This money helps build and repair the
trucks. It also helps pay for the salaries of
mechanics and drivers. It helps with traveling
costs.

**Sponsors put their names on the monster trucks they
help support.**

In return for the money, sponsors get their names and logos painted on the trucks. Supporting a popular truck is good advertising for a business. Auto companies, fuel suppliers, banks, garages, tire makers, and other businesses like their logos to be seen at truck rallies.

Sponsors want to be thought of as the choice of the champions. Then they can sell more of their products to both monster-truck drivers and monster-truck fans.

Supporting a popular truck is good advertising for a business.

Chapter 4

Safety First

When monster trucks first started racing, some drivers hung out of their windows when crushing cars. This was dangerous. So the Monster Truck Racing Association (MTRA) was formed in the late 1980s. It set safety rules. The MTRA makes sure all trucks follow the rules.

Monster truck racing is very safe. Drivers no longer hang out the windows. Seat belts hold the drivers firmly in place. Drivers wear helmets, fire-resistant suits, and fireproof gloves. Firefighters and paramedics are always ready at events.

Before the Monster Truck Drag Racing Association set rules, some monster truck drivers were not very safe.

Spectators Protected

Promoters and drivers do everything they can to protect the fans. Shields stop truck parts and pieces from flying around after crashes. Nylon blankets are wrapped around the **transmissions** in case they explode.

Every truck has a kill switch. If a truck gets out of control, a driver can use the switch to stop the truck. Some trucks have remote control kill switches. Team members can turn the engine off from the sidelines.

Some events are held outside. Then rain can make the roofs of the junk cars slippery. Drivers cannot see what their tires are doing. They have to feel where the truck is going.

Experience

Experience is what makes many drivers safe. Leaping high over a row of cars might look exciting. But the fastest way over the obstacles is to keep low. It is also the safest way. It takes practice to drive well.

Drivers have to feel where their trucks are going. Experience is what makes a driver safest.

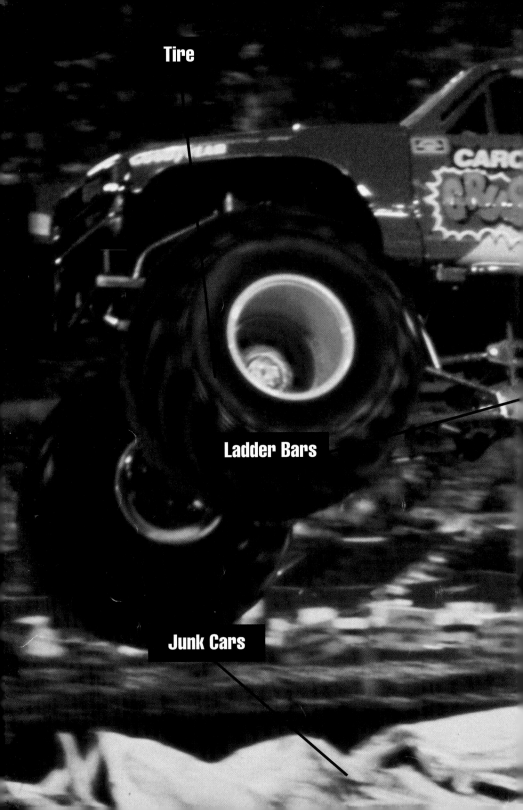

Tire

Ladder Bars

Junk Cars

Shock Absorber

Body

The best drivers help the **pit** crew when there are problems. The pit crew are the mechanics who keep the trucks running.

Monster trucks can go as fast as 55 miles (88 kilometers) per hour. That might not seem very fast. But it is very fast for the stunts done by monster trucks. If the trucks went any faster, there would probably be more accidents and more injuries.

Drivers and crews from different teams get together after the races. They see each other at events all across North America. They are friendly competitors.

In the pits, fans can see monster trucks close-up.

Glossary

custom-made—made to fit a special order
disqualify—kick out of a race
heat—preliminary rounds of a race
pit—area away from the track where mechanics work on trucks
promoter—person who organizes a race
rally—vehicle competition
roll cage—tubes welded together that surround the driver and protect against injury
shock absorber—tube-shaped device that absorbs bumps
supercharger—system that pumps vaporized fuel to make a vehicle go faster
terrain—a piece of land or ground
traction—the ability of something to grip a surface
transmission—gears that transfer power from the engine to the wheels
wheelie—vehicle rearing up on its back wheels

Dangerous Toy is one of many names people have chosen for their monster trucks.

To Learn More

Atkinson, E.J. *Monster Vehicles*. Mankato, Minn.: Capstone Press, 1989.

Brazier, Barry. *Monster-Mobile*. Park, Calif.: Haynes Publications, 1987.

Connolly, Maureen. *Dragsters*. Mankato, Minn.: Capstone Press, 1992.

Holder, Bill. *The Ultimate Book of Monster Trucks*. Greenwich, Conn.: Brompton Books, 1991.

Holder, Bill and Harry Dunn. *Monster Wheels*. New York: Sterling Publishing, 1990.

Johnston, Scott D. *Monster Truck Racing*. Minneapolis: Capstone Press, 1994.

Grave Digger is another popular monster truck.

Useful Addresses

Bigfoot 4x4
6311 North Lindbergh Boulevard
St. Louis, MO 63042

Carolina Crusher
P.O. Box 151
Wadesboro, NC 28170

SRO Motorsports (Promoter)
477 East Butterfield Road
Suite 400
Lombard, IL 60148

United Sport of America
(Promotes Canadian Events)
2310 West 75th Street
Prairie Village, KS 66208

Monster trucks can bounce in the air when they go over rows of junk cars.

Internet Sites

America's 4x4 4U Video Magazine
http://www.4x44u.com/pub/k2/am4x44u/
4x4.htm

Bigfoot
http://www.bigfoot4x4.com

Monster Trucks
http://www.trader.com/users/9675/6589/
monster.htm

NHRA Online
http://www.goracing.com/nhra/

TruckWorld
http://www.truckworld.com/

Many monster-truck rallies are held at indoor stadiums.

Index